THE MAN

AS A LE

THE MANAGER
AS A LEADER

by Colin Chase

The Industrial Society

First published 1969 by
The Industrial Society
Robert Hyde House
48 Bryanston Square
London W1H 7LN
Telephone: 0171 479 2000

Eighth edition, July 1990
© *The Industrial Society. 1969, 1983, 1989*
Reprinted 1991, 1999

ISBN 0 85290 431 2

British Library Cataloguing in Publication Data
Chase, Colin
    The manager as a leader.—7th ed.
    1. Management. Leadership
    I. Title II. Chase, Colin III. Industrial Society
    IV. Series
    658.4'092

Printed and bound in Great Britain by QSR, Loughborough

CONTENTS

1

MANAGEMENT OR

LEADERSHIP?

Leadership is fashionable, and good leaders are recognised as being those in management that really make things happen, rather than those who simply administer. We have witnessed the leadership abilities of those that have turned around giants like ICI, British Steel, Rolls Royce and British Airways, whilst others have achieved much the same but on a smaller scale. These are the smaller business people, and also the leaders of management buyouts. They may not have the national profile of corporate leaders, but their leadership abilities are still vital to their organisation's success in today's international market place.

Yet the efforts of all these top leaders would be to no avail without the applied leadership abilities of all those in charge, at every level of their organisations. As a former chairman of British Steel expressed it: 'however grand the driver's intentions, the only thing that matters is where "the rubber meets the road".'

It is therefore vital that we seek to understand leadership so that those in a position of authority (at any level) can be trained on how they achieve results with people.

It is no longer good enough to operate on a basis of fear. We live in the age of communication, where we expect to know what is happening; to be part of the action; to have a say in the affairs of the society we live in and the organisation we work in. Somehow, those expectations have to be matched to the requirements of the organisation so that there is a sharing of vision and achievement of common purpose.

Definition of leadership

How, then, can we define leadership in order to develop the abilities of those in charge of others? First, we must understand the basis of any manager's job. This can be described as being within three skill areas.

1 *Technical.* A manager must have sufficient technical competence to know what to expect from others and be able to recognise when the job is of the right quality and when it is below standard. It is seldom necessary to be technically excellent, thereby having the ability to carry out the technical context of a job better than any individual team member. This issue will be addressed again later.

2 *Administration.* It is necessary to understand the methods and procedures that are the administrative framework of the organisation. It is then possible to both maintain the standards of these procedures and be a champion for changing those that no longer suit the needs of the current operation. Again, it is not necessary to be the administrative expert.

3 *Achieving results through people.* This is the focus of leadership which begins to stand 'leaders' apart from 'managers'. We do not administer people, nor do we get others to do only those jobs that we don't want to do. As the Chief Executive of British Aerospace put it: 'leadership is the art of getting more from people than they think they are capable of giving'.

Identifying the ability

How then do we identify and develop our leadership abilities? There have traditionally been three different approaches, though there are many 'schools' that can be identified within each. The main divisions are:

- qualities or traits
- situational
- functional.

Qualities or traits

Any team will expect its leader to have certain qualities, which invariably will differ with individual perceptions. Numerous lists have been carefully drawn up, particularly by those seeking to identify leadership potential for the armed forces. Field Marshal Lord Slim achieved the shortest list: courage; willpower; initiative; knowledge. Lord Harding added integrity, fitness, judgement, and team spirit.

There may be a sense of discomfort about some of these qualities and traits: for example, the level of fitness to be attained, or the amount of initiative required. However, these are the briefest lists of qualities. The Royal Canadian Mounted Police, for example, seek 18 qualities that include humour, honesty, good judgement, and decisiveness.

Clearly, it is dangerous to select leaders solely by virtue of their qualities because of the different appeal and interpretations of such things as 'humour' or 'honesty'. It would be doubtful whether such an approach would allow us to achieve agreement on the factors sought and the method of identifying them. Even then, it provides little scope for training and development.

The best we can do is identify the individual strengths of people that have a common accord, and seek to maximise these. For example, the leader who is seen to be fit and energetic may well be more suited to a particular type of job or organisation. In this way, we can at least acknowledge the strengths in each individual without assessing all potential leaders under one set of quality criteria and thereby establishing a 'have got' or 'have not got' leadership ability. One result of this is the assessment category of 'not yet a born leader'.

Situational

Two main schools emerge from this approach to leadership. The first is based on having the leader most suited to the immediate situation. This can happen through either the natural leader arising from the group according to the activity, or the group appointing that leader through consensus. In either event, we do not have a practical solution to managing at work, where the leader is appointed by those above. Yet many organisations unwittingly tread this path, by the way they promote the best secretary to be the office supervisor; the outstanding sales person to be the sales manager; or the reliable accountant to be the accounts manager. Little wonder that, without training in leadership skill, the department flounders.

Leaders must have the technical competence to recognise the standards and quality in their organisation necessary to meet customer requirements, but there is more to it. Leaders must have the necessary understanding and skill for their position of having to get work done through and with other people.

The second 'situational' school is based on leaders adapting their style to meet the situation in which they find themselves. This can apply to both the organisational activities (e.g. fast growth, retrenchment, start up, diversification) and the individual's capabilities (e.g. experienced, fresh in job, fast-track). Its strength is in the recognition that leaders should be aware of what is going on around them and take such observations into account. The weakness is that it can be difficult to identify sufficiently, and accurately, the style necessary for any particular situation without resulting in a confused workforce.

Functional

This approach concentrates on the actions a leader must take to be successful. From this premise of concentrating on the leadership functions of management, a number of different schools have arisen, each seeking to encapsulate a range of activities within a simple framework or model. One of the most practical and established is that describing the leader as existing to get a job done through the efforts of individual human beings working as a team.

As a result, there would appear to be three inter-related areas in which to work:

- ensuring that the required TASKS are continually achieved
- building and reinforcing the TEAM and fostering TEAMWORK and TEAM SPIRIT
- developing each INDIVIDUAL member of the team.

2

ACTION-CENTRED

LEADERSHIP

Taking this functional approach to leadership, we can focus on the actions required which are relevant to any level of management. This has become an organisational philosophy for companies in search of excellence. This approach is based on the three areas of work, with each influencing the other:

- achieving the TASK
- building the TEAM
- developing INDIVIDUALS.

This can be illustrated with the simple model of Action-Centred Leadership (Fig. 1).

Fig. 1.

The leader is not a part of the team, but is a member of his/her own peer group and, as such, is engaged in tasks as a team member at that level of management. Invariably, this level will have longer time horizons, larger financial responsibilities, and more significant decisions impacting on employees and customers. From this position, the leader should stand back in order to be able to monitor progress towards desired results through the activities of individuals, and also the extent of teamwork. The effective leader then evaluates what is learnt and acts accordingly, with praise or corrective measures. For example, it may be necessary to become part of the team in providing an extra pair of hands, or additional brain power. The skill is to know when to stand back again before being accused of 'interfering'. Of course, the leader who is seldom visible and rarely supports the team will be accused of 'not caring'—so observation and evaluation are vital in determining the right balance.

Putting it into practice

Considering this in a little more detail, we will first examine the integration of the three circles by an effective leader.

Achieving the task and objectives

The need to accomplish the tasks for which the team, unit, department and, indeed, organisation exists, is the primary and most obvious duty of the manager. A leader who consistently fails to achieve targets and budgets is unlikely to remain a leader for very long! However, we must also accept that never to fail is probably never to take risks—in today's changing world, that is a balance every manager must continually be assessing if they are to be a leader. It is therefore vital to be clear about what our objectives are, how we are going to achieve our tasks, and to what standards.

However, in their zeal to reach the objective for which they are responsible, managers will too often yield to the temptation to 'do it themselves'. The chief engineer will use the tools the engineers should be using; the chief chemist cannot resist finishing the delicate crystallisation on which so many month's experiments depend. They may actually be capable of doing it better, but it is not the job of the leader. Managers that find themselves doing these things more than occasionally should stop and consider why.

Building and maintaining a winning team

Although we are employed by organisations on the basis of individual contracts, it is in teams that the majority of our work is conducted—in the office, the purchasing section, the 'twilight' shift, the 'heavy' gang, or on a project. These teams exist because the task cannot be achieved by one person alone. Neither can it be most effectively achieved by a 'group' of people. In too many organisations there are groups that lack teamwork, particularly where complex organisational structures are used.

It is the leader's responsibility to build teamwork by directing each individual's efforts towards the achievement of the organisation's objectives. The leader must consciously set about gaining the loyalty of members to the team, their pride in belonging, their desire to work together as a team, and the standards they accept.

Teams differ from groups because in teams, each individual understands and values the contribution of the other members. They work to a common goal—some people call it 'group synergy'. The leader should also make effective use of the energy which will arise in the team by listening to the ideas generated. Clear decisions are then taken regarding which ideas are to be used and how and why others are not currently being pursued.

We can therefore see how much the 'team circle' overlaps the 'task circle'.

Developing individuals

We must not forget that all members of the team need to continue to live and express themselves as individuals; to provide for those dependent upon them; to find satisfaction in their work and play. In order to satisfy these needs, people must exert themselves—they must get involved. Fortunately for the manager, there is a high coincidence between these needs and the management obligation to achieve results through the best use of resources—in this case, human.

The leader must ensure that individuals: know what is expected of them; feel they are making a significant and worthwhile contribution to the task; and receive adequate recognition for it.

Ideally, every job should: draw out the best from each human being; use abilities; match responsibilities to capabilities; stretch; challenge and enable people to grow. An individual should be able to look back and think 'a year ago, I would have been really worried about doing this job, and now I'm taking it in my stride'.

Occasionally, the leader may need to help or counsel individuals over some problem which is new, unfamiliar, or even daunting.

If the leader does not develop, or pay sufficient attention to, individuals then they may withdraw from the team. They may be at work, but not working.

Keeping a balance of action

It is the leader's responsibility to take action in all three areas. However, circumstances will not always allow equal attention to be paid to all three areas. There will be occasions when all of your energies will be devoted to achieving the task (e.g. during a period of crisis or when there is a rush job to complete). But whenever that vital period is past, it is important to reassess the impact of that action on individuals and teamwork. This may simply be a case of acknowledging the efforts made during the crisis with a well meant 'thank you'.

The interaction of these areas can also be seen when a department or project is continually failing to achieve targets. Team morale tends to drop and individual reaction can turn to apathy or aggression. Equally, if the team is torn by internal dissension and jealousies, its performance, as well as individual satisfaction, will suffer. This can identify itself in absenteeism, staff turnover, poor timekeeping, and a general fall in standards. It is quite false to address ourselves to these 'problem' people—it is to their manager that we should be looking for corrective action.

Task orientation

Poor leadership can also be seen through over-identification with one area of activity. Consider the manager who is continuously 'task orientated'. This can be represented by Fig. 2.

Fig. 2

The 'task master' is driven by the figures—always striving to improve performance by whatever financial or technical criterion is considered most appropriate. Little attention is paid to team members as human beings that have consider-able responsibilities of their own outside of work. Neither will teamwork play a very large part in this leader's approach. In today's climate of shorter working hours, longer leisure time, and greater amenities, this leader will indeed have little commitment from his or her people. They will do their best to keep out of trouble, looking forward to their income for the ability to pursue life outside of work. Little creativity will be ssen here, apart from getting around management rules. Money will become an increasingly prime motivator, with management responding in numerous ingenious incentive schemes—which probably breed greater discontent. Frequently a symptom of the organisation basing its managerial promotion on technical criteria at the expense of leadership potential.

Team orientation

Then there is the leader who wants to be seen as one of the team and be 'popular'. So we see distortion as represented by Fig. 3.

Fig. 3.

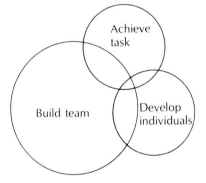

Leaders have to take difficult decisions, many of which may be unpopular. Indeed, it would be most worrying if all management decisions were popular. By identifying so closely with the team, the leader is unlikely to take timely corrective action if, for instance, standards of customer service are failing or discipline dropping. The longer these things are left unchecked, the more difficult it will be to face up to them. On the one hand, the leader is trying to work hard at team spirit. On the other hand, through misguided action, the leader is failing to maintain individual standards, is not achieving the task, and morale is flagging. A really severe case of 'over identification with the team'. This can be a particular problem when the leader has been selected from within the team and not been given sufficient leadership training to cope with the changing position.

Concentrating on individuals

Finally, there is the manager who concentrates on a few individuals in the team. This is represented by Fig. 4.

Fig. 4.

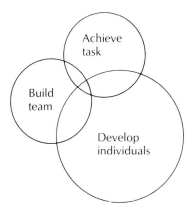

At one extreme are those individuals receiving the majority of the leader's attention, possibly because they are 'high fliers'. They benefit from particularly demanding or challenging assignments so that others seldom have the opportunity to equally demonstrate their abilities. At the other extreme are those gaining the leader's attention through lack of skills or ability, resulting in undue support by the leader, or even excessive monitoring and disciplining.

As equal opportunities become a more established part of company culture, there will be a need to make even greater efforts to balance individual development with team building and task accomplishment. Excessive attention to someone in the team of different sex, colour, religion, age, or disability, could well result in dissension or jealousy which will affect overall performance.

3

LEADERSHIP PROCESSES

We now need to identify the processes that will help us towards leading that winning team. To win, we can determine five key stages in the process.

1 *Defining the objectives.* Being clear what is required in quantitative and qualitative terms.

2 *Planning.* To meet these objectives. This will almost certainly involve two phases.
   - Gathering of information, ideas and suggestions. This is the phase that will probably demand management activity in collecting relevant data, and a leadership approach to the involvement of others through gaining ideas and suggestions. There are many aspects to these activities, broadly grouped under 'consultative' processes (e.g. quality circles, task forces, advisory committees, staff councils).
   - Taking the decision. This must have clarity of timing so that everyone understands that the consultative phase is complete and that minds are not focused on actually getting the work done (*see Decision Taking,* in this series).

3 *Briefing.* It is vital that everyone understands the plan so that teamwork is part of the process from the beginning. The leader briefs the team, checks for understanding and gains commitment to the work ahead.

4 *Monitor and support.* In achieving results through people, the leader has now created the environment for individuals to work willingly and well at what needs to be done. Standing back is a vital part of the leadership

function. Yet we also find that if you stand back too far and are seldom seen, then the team is likely to consider that you do not support, or are not particularly interested in, their work. Visible leadership, 'management by walking about', or, as The Industrial Society prefers to call it: 'Walking the Job', so that you observe, listen, and learn, is extremely important.

5   *Evaluate.* Walking the job is not a fitness exercise. It is learning by listening and seeing, so that we can decide what follow-up action needs to take place. It is quite possible that we may wish to modify our aims; alternatively, perhaps we haven't achieved what we set out to achieve. In such cases, if we are to meet original specifications, it is almost certain that we will want to return to the planning process.

These five key stages could be viewed as an action cycle (see Fig. 5).

Fig. 5.

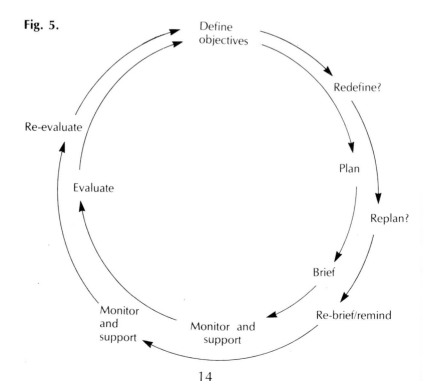

This cycle represents both small, or relatively easy tasks, and the more major tasks or overall objectives. In developing the leadership process for a major task or project, constraints may be identified at an early stage without ever reaching the briefing stage. Similarly, having planned, we might be briefing the team when, as a result of questioning, it becomes clear that some aspect of the plan is seriously flawed. It could be argued that this should have been identified during the gathering of information and consultative processes. But it would be a foolish leader who ignores such a flaw and carries on with the original plan. As visible leadership strikes a balance between 'spying' and 'not caring', the desire to admit that you are not always right has to be balanced with being indecisive. If a plan needs modification at first briefing, then it is because it is *not going to work*, rather than because it could be *slightly better*. So we can modify our action cycle as in Fig. 6.

Fig. 6.

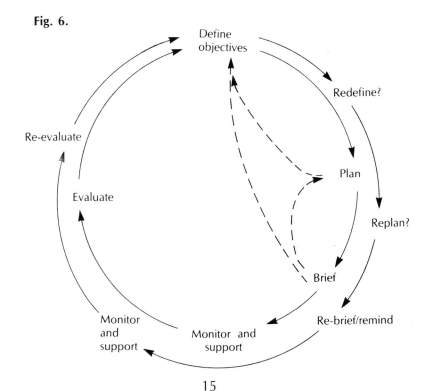

It is by following these leadership actions of defining the objectives, consulting, deciding, briefing, followed by supporting, monitoring, and evaluating against objectives, that identifies the manager as a leader.

4

FRAMEWORK FOR

LEADERSHIP

We can now bring the action cycle together with the three-circle model in order to identify our framework for leadership.

Our framework (see Fig. 7) relates the three job areas to the key processes so that actions can be identified. These actions are so inter-related that their position in one part of the framework does not mean that they do not have relevance in another. However, for practical purposes they have been grouped under the area to which they *mainly* relate.

Checklist—achieving the task

The leader's main contributions to achieving the task lie in:

- being quite clear about what the task is, putting it over with enthusiasm, and reminding people of it often
- understanding how the task fits into the overall short- and long-term objectives of the organisation
- planning how to accomplish it
- defining and providing the resources needed, including the time and the authority required
- doing everything possible to ensure the organisational structure allows the task to be done efficiently
- pacing progress towards achievement of the task
- evaluating results and comparing them with the original plans and the objectives of the organisation.

Fig. 7. Framework for leadership

KEY ACTIONS		TASK	TEAM	INDIVIDUAL
Define objectives		Identify tasks & constraints	Hold team meetings / Share commitment	Clarify objectives / Gain acceptance
Plan	Gather information	Consider Options / Check resources	Consult / Develop suggestions	Encourage ideas / Assess skills
	Decide	Priorities / Time scales / Standards	Structure	Allocate jobs / Delegate / Set Targets
Brief		Clarify objectives / Describe plan	Explain decisions / Answer questions / Check understanding	Listen / Enthuse
Monitor Support		Assess progress / Maintain standards	Coordinate / Reconcile conflict	Advise / Assist/reassure / Counsel discipline
			Recognise effort	
Evaluate		Summarise / Review objectives / Replan if necessary	Recognise & gain from success / Learn from mistakes	Appraise performance
			Guide & train	Give praise

Checklist—building the team

The key actions of the leader in building the team are to:

- set and maintain the team's objectives and standards
- involve the team as a whole in the achievement of objectives
- maintain the unity of the team by seeing that dissident activity is minimised
- communicate regularly with the team face-to-face, at least once a month, on matters of people, policy, progress, and points for action
- consult with the team, whenever time permits, before taking decisions which affect them
- explain the organisation's results and achievements
- communicate any changes taking place in the organisation and how they will affect the team.

Checklist—developing individuals

A leader must be aware of how to get people to work willingly and well, so as to increase the individual's satisfaction in the job, and the organisation's efficiency.

Every leader must:

Provide a challenge and scope for development by:

- setting targets, after consulting, and reviewing them at regular intervals
- providing relevant training—where appropriate by using people to train others, in the specialist skills they may have
- arranging any necessary internal and external contact
- restructuring or grouping tasks to use people's skill to the fullest
- rotating jobs to broaden experience

- providing scope for individuals to take greater responsibility
- training thoroughly at least one deputy.

Make people feel valued by:

- knowing their name, their place of work, and interests outside of work
- regularly monitoring and appreciating individual effort
- sharing an interest in whatever they hold important
- creating a good working environment by being approachable
- ensuring everyone understands the importance of their contribution to the team's objectives
- ensuring everyone understands the function of the organisation.

Recognise achievements by:

- praising and communicating individual successes
- holding regular meetings with each individual to monitor and counsel
- providing guidance for a personal development programme
- operating a fair and open policy of linking salary to performance.

Providing the right climate and opportunities for these needs to be met for each individual in the team is possibly the most difficult, and certainly the most challenging and rewarding part of the leader's responsibilities.

Checklists—leadership action cycle

Defining objectives

For the leader to define objectives, it is necessary to consider:

- how they relate to the longer-term objectives of the organisation
- limits of own authority
- financial limits of authority
- time constraints at key stages of the task
- what our competitors are doing
- whether there will be conflict with other departments—if so, how it should be minimised
- the skills available
- whether the physical working conditions (equipment, heat, light, layout) will be appropriate for the job
- how jobs can be designed to encourage the commitment of individuals and the team
- when to hold a team meeting to brief on the objective.

Planning

GATHERING INFORMATION

The leader will need to check the following points.

- Any potential gaps in the abilities of the team (including the leader) that are needed in order to achieve any of the tasks. If necessary, identify what steps need to be taken to fill them by training, by additional staff, or by the use of specialists.
- Availability of necessary resources—manpower, money, materials, methods, machinery, and time.
- Whether consultation is appropriate. If so, check that the team have been briefed on the objectives and that an agenda has been issued.
- What steps can be taken to encourage new ideas from the team (e.g. brainstorming, task group, quality circles).
- What regular opportunities are provided for genuine consultation with the team before taking decisions affecting them (e.g. work plans, output, methods, changing places of work, hours, or reporting lines).
- Who outside the immediate team should be involved.

DECIDING

The leader should ensure that:

- all the options have been considered within the time-scale set
- everyone knows the time and place of the next team meeting at which decisions are to be communicated
- everyone knows exactly what their job is
- each individual has clearly defined targets and performance standards, set following consultation
- everyone knows by name to whom they are accountable, and will be in teams of 4–8 if professional staff, and in any case no more than 15
- arrangements have been made for continuity of leadership in leader's absence
- the degree of delegation (e.g. sign their own letters, write the monthly report, do the next presentation, take the queries on a particular subject, project or profit area) is currently at the maximum
- the decision and plan is recorded in writing.

Briefing

The leader will be identified and 'measured' more by the way he or she communicates, than by any other single factor. It is vital to:

- get all the team together regularly
- explain decisions and gain commitment
- brief those outside your team through their bosses
- put across the plan with enthusiasm
- set objectives for the team that are understood by everyone
- encourage questions and provide feedback for those questions to which the answers are not already known
- listen to people's questions and comments

- read the communication signals from facial expressions and body postures
- confirm the briefing in writing.

Monitoring and supporting

Visible leadership is about:

- regularly walking the job by visiting each person's place of work to observe, listen and praise
- knowing the names and titles of all in the team—and using them
- smiling and saying: 'Good morning' with meaning
- being aware of just how the team and leader are managing time; looking for the best way to do so and ensuring that priorities are right
- ensuring that your own work and behaviour standards set the best possible example to the team
- knowing enough about the members of the team to enable you to have an accurate picture of their aptitudes and attitudes at work
- looking for better ways to design jobs, or arranging work to make the best use of people's aptitudes, skills and interest, in order to involve them and gain their commitment
- giving sufficient time and personal attention to matters of direct concern to the individual—their development, training and, where relevant, social and recreational opportunities
- seeing that the team is clear about the working standards expected from them, e.g. in timekeeping, quality of work, housekeeping, safety. 'Having a go' at those who break them
- looking for opportunities for building teamwork into jobs
- checking that there is a formal and fair grievance procedure understood by all, and that the leader deals with grievances and complaints promptly.

Evaluating

Defining the team's direction, planning and briefing, and leading visibly, is to no avail unless the leader allocates time to thinking and evaluating against the original objectives.

- Are the objectives being achieved? If so, are there any individual or team contributions to acknowledge? If not, do the objectives have to be redefined, or does the plan need revising? What authority do I have in these areas?

- In the event of success, do I acknowledge it and build on it? In the case of failure, do I criticise constructively and give guidance on improving future performance?

- Do I design jobs or arrange work to make the best use of peoples' aptitudes, skills and interest, in order to involve them and gain their commitment?

- Can I remove some controls, while retaining my account-ability? For example, can I cut down on the amount of checking I do by holding subordinates more and more responsible for the quality and accuracy of their work?

- Can I delegate more decisions to individuals?

- Has each individual a continuing list of short-term targets for the improvement of their performance, each with its own maturity date?

- Have I made adequate provision for the training and (where necessary) retraining of each person?

- Is the overall performance of each individual regularly (at least annually) reviewed in face-to-face discussion?

- Do I take action on matters likely to disrupt the team, e.g. unjustified differentials in pay, uneven workloads, availability of information technology, discrepancies in the distribution of overtime?

- Do I care for the well-being of the team and seek to improve their working conditions?

- Am I sure that for each individual, work, capacity, and pay are in balance?

- Does the individual see some pattern of career – and salary – development? And if someone is about to retire, do they need help in meeting the problems of retirement?

- If, after opportunities for training and development, someone is still not meeting the requirements of the job, do I try to find a position for them more nearly matching their capacity—or see that someone else does?

- Is the human resource planning correct, or will I need to start redefining recruitment, selection, and training needs? Do I really have an equal opportunities policy that is seen to be working?

- Do all team leaders get a minimum of three day's leadership training a year?

5

BY DOING,

ONE BECOMES

In summary, the job of a leader at any level is to:

- get the required results (ACHIEVE TASK)
- build an effective and cohesive team (BUILD TEAM)
- 'grow' and develop each individual, and provide the satisfaction of having a valued member of an effective team (DEVELOP INDIVIDUALS).

These are the actions of a leader. This is the 'work' a manager has to perform to be a successful leader. They are not inborn traits. They are skills which can be recognised, practised and developed.

What distinguishes the leader at each level is the timescale by which results are planned, and the impact they have on the number of individuals. The higher the level, the greater these factors should be.

To help build and develop the talents we all have, we can use this book as a source of well-proven practical tools of leadership. What we need to do is to work hard with these tools in our own way, without trying to suppress our own natural character or inclinations, or worrying whether our personality is appropriate. The rest will follow.

The entire emphasis is on the actions leaders take, upon what they DO rather than the sort of people they are. It has been shown time and time again that by DOING, one BECOMES a more effective leader.